Introduction: What is a river? 2
1 The water cycle 4
2 Beginnings and ends 6
3 Drainage areas 8
4 Rivers at work 10
5 River valleys and waterfalls 14
6 Flood plains 20
7 Mysterious meanders 22
8 Deltas and estuaries 24
9 Rivers and industry 26
10 Enjoying rivers 28
11 Controlling rivers 30
12 Looking at a local river 32
13 Some great world rivers 36
Conclusion: Why are rivers so important to us? 44
Glossary 46
Index 48

Introduction

What is a river?

In this book you will find out about different rivers. You will investigate how they work and how they change the landscape. You will find out how we can use rivers to help us, and learn about the problems they can create. No two rivers are exactly the same, but the very longest river and the smallest stream have things in common.

Some of the world's great rivers

As you read this book you will come across words in **bold** type describing how rivers work. The Glossary on pages 46 and 47 explains these for you.

Things to do

- Make a list of five things that describe a river.

As you read and use this book you will find out the answer to this question:

Why are rivers so important to us?

Things to do

Look carefully at the photos on these pages. Make two lists:

- How are the rivers alike?
- How are they different?

3

The water cycle

Three-quarters, or 75 per cent, of the Earth's surface is covered by water.

There is water in the oceans and seas, in lakes and ponds. It flows in rivers and streams. Ice in glaciers and icebergs is also a form of water.

Only a very small part of the Earth's water is fresh. Most of it (97 per cent) is found in oceans and seas, and is salty.

All living things – plants and animals – need water to survive. Humans use more water than any other animal.

Why do we never run out of water?

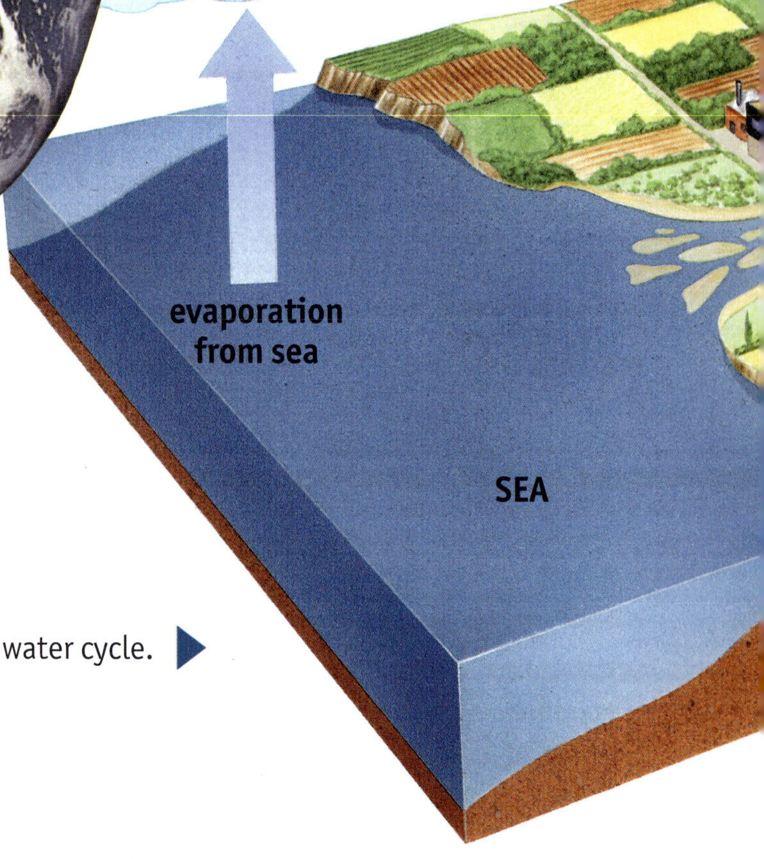

evaporation from sea

SEA

A diagram of the water cycle. ▶

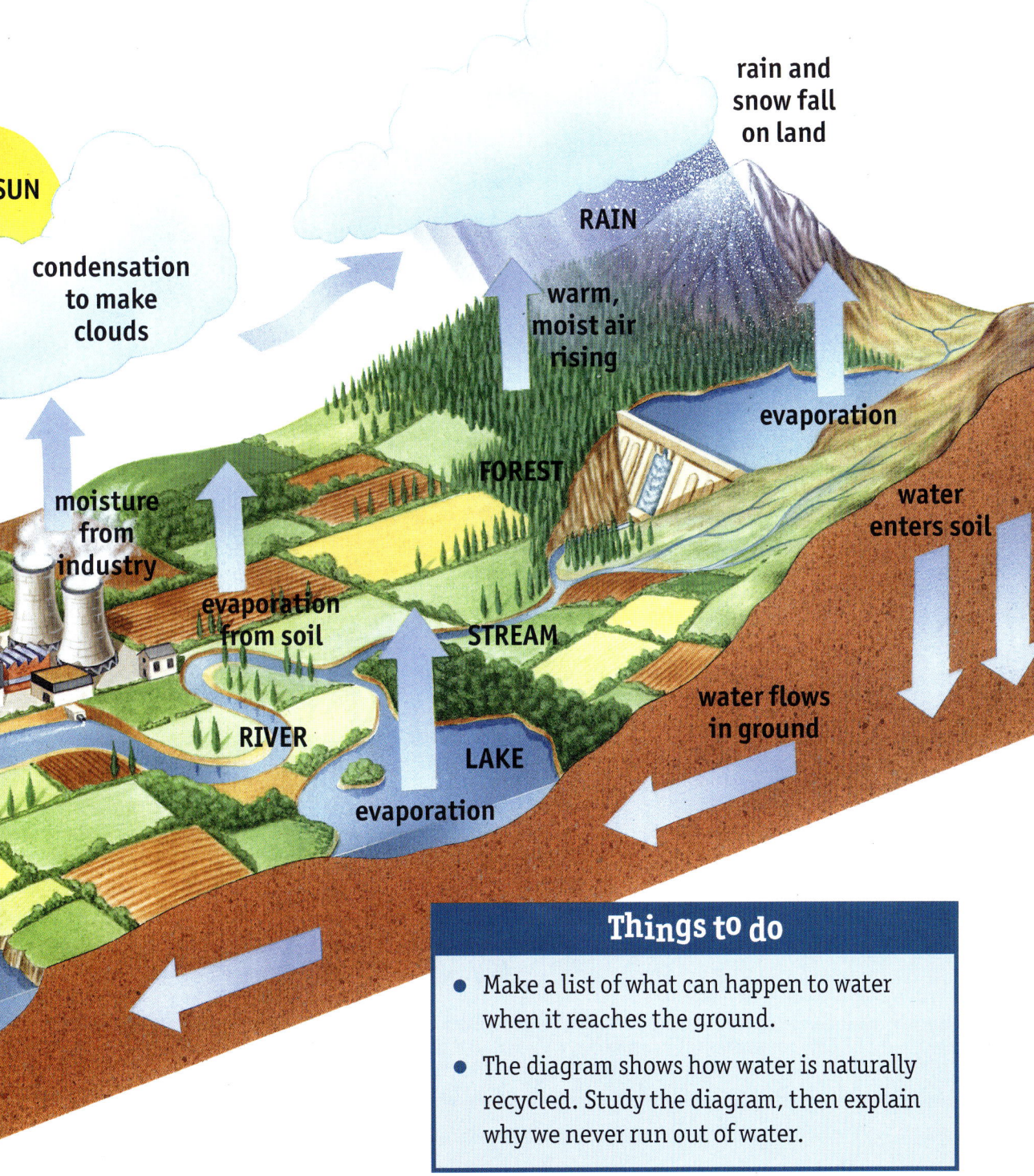

Things to do

- Make a list of what can happen to water when it reaches the ground.
- The diagram shows how water is naturally recycled. Study the diagram, then explain why we never run out of water.

Beginnings and ends

How do rivers start?

The start of a river is called its **source**.

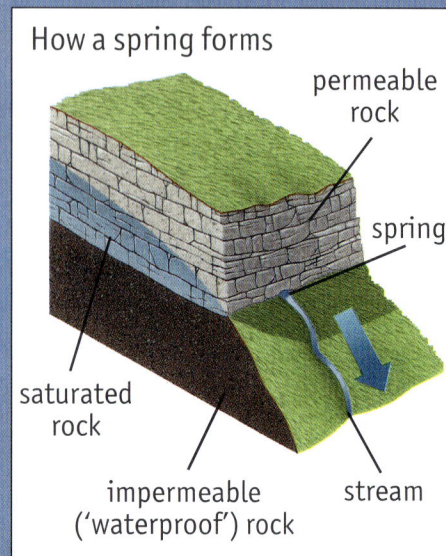

How a spring forms — permeable rock, spring, saturated rock, impermeable ('waterproof') rock, stream

Water is able to soak into some sorts of rock. These are called **permeable** rocks. If the water meets a layer of 'waterproof' or **impermeable** rocks which it cannot sink through, then the rock above becomes saturated (full of water). Where the saturated rock meets the surface, a stream is formed.

Think about

Look back at the picture of the water cycle on pages 4–5, which shows what happens to rainwater when it reaches the ground.

- What else could start a stream flowing?

How do rivers finish?

These three maps show the ends or **mouths** of three different rivers. One joins another river, one goes into a lake, and the other flows into the sea. Which is which?

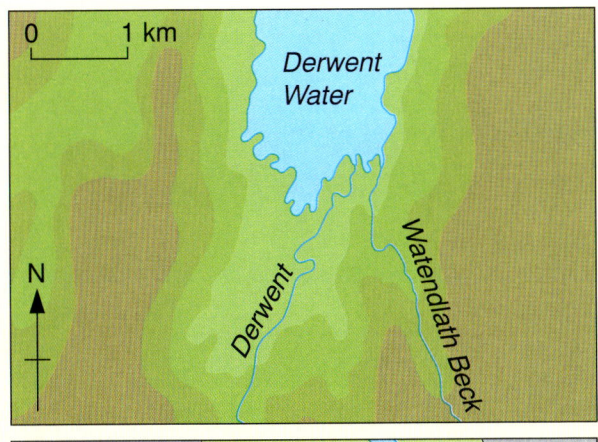

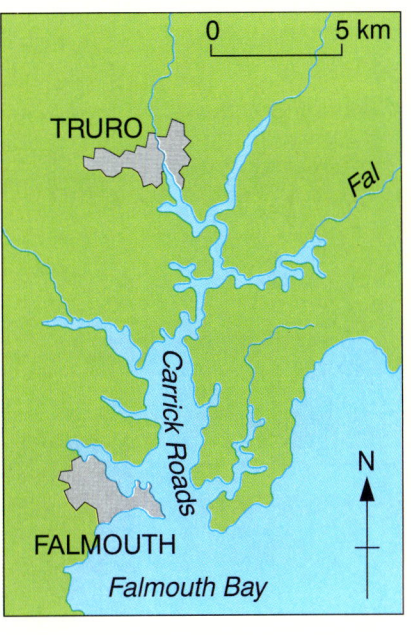

Things to do

Find an atlas map showing the rivers in Africa. Make three lists of some African rivers to show how they finish:

Rivers joining other rivers	Rivers flowing into a lake	Rivers flowing into the sea

Drainage areas

Why are rivers different?

These rivers are both in Britain. Each photo is taken about halfway between the source of the river and its mouth. The area of land across which the water flows is called a **river basin** or **drainage area**.

Think about

- How do these two rivers look different?

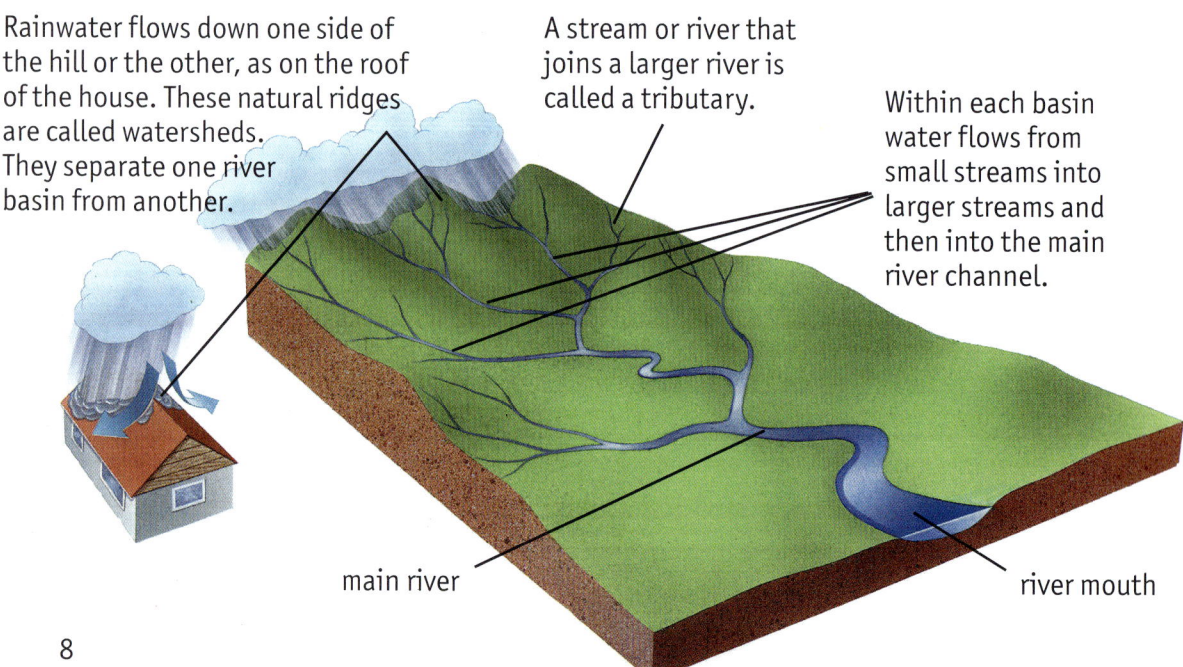

Rainwater flows down one side of the hill or the other, as on the roof of the house. These natural ridges are called watersheds. They separate one river basin from another.

A stream or river that joins a larger river is called a tributary.

Within each basin water flows from small streams into larger streams and then into the main river channel.

main river

river mouth

8

◀ The River Rhine basin is one of the largest river basins in Europe.

Things to find

- How many countries are there in the Rhine basin?
- How many countries does the river flow through?
- Find out which are the two largest river basins in Europe.
- Find out which is the largest river basin in the world.
- What is the world's longest river?
- Are the answers to the last two questions the same?

Things to do

The drainage area of each river is different. Look at this list. Which points mean that the river is likely to be large and powerful? Which mean the river is more likely to be smaller and gently flowing?
- large basin/small basin
- impermeable (waterproof) rocks/permeable rocks
- lots of trees/few trees
- wet climate/dry climate
- steep slope/gentle slope

Now try to explain the differences you can see in the two rivers pictured on page 8.

4 Rivers at work

Water is a very powerful force, and rivers play an important part in shaping the landscape.

How do rivers change the landscape?

Rivers change the landscape in three ways: by erosion, by transportation and by **deposition**.

Erosion
Water is able to wear away soil and rock particles from the bed and banks of rivers. This process is called **erosion**. The amount that a river erodes depends on how much force or energy it has. A river shapes its own channel by erosion, deepening and widening it as it moves along.

▼ The three main sorts of river erosion

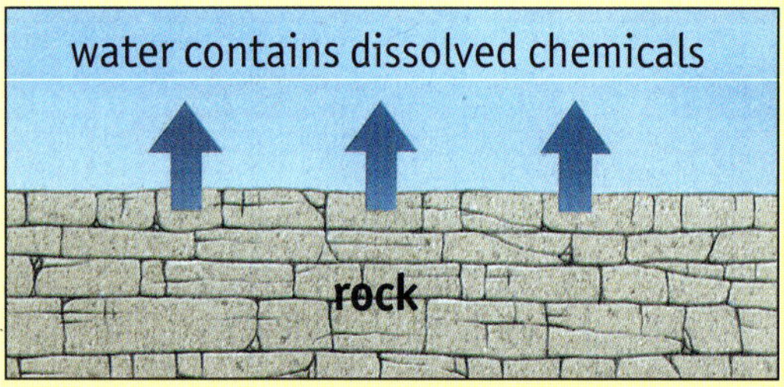

Think about

Why might the three sorts of erosion vary in importance:
- from one river to another
- in different parts of the same river
- at different times of the year?

Hydraulic erosion ▶
Water is forced into cracks in the river bed. This dislodges lumps of rock which are moved downstream.

◀ **Chemical erosion**
Rivers contain chemicals that have been dissolved by the water. Some sorts of rock, like limestone, dissolve more easily than others, like granite.

◀ **Physical erosion**
A river carries material such as sand and stones. These grind along the river bed and erode more of the river channel.

10

Transportation

Material carried by the river, such as sand and stones, is called the **load**. The amount of load in a river depends on how much material has been eroded by the water, and how much has been washed into the river from the surrounding land. The water carries the load downstream. This process is called **transportation**.

The load can be transported in three ways:
1 *in solution:* this means that materials are dissolved in the water.
2 *in suspension:* light materials, like **silt** and sand, are carried along with the water.
3 *as bed load:* larger stones and even boulders are rolled along the river bed by the force of the water.

▲ A clear stream flowing over limestone rock

▲ A river with very muddy water

Think about

- How do you think most of the river's load is transported in each of these photos?
- Which type of transportation do you think moves the greatest load in a river? Why do you think this?

▲ A fast-flowing mountain stream

A similar view of the Ouse at York at different times of the year

Think about

- What differences can you see between these two pictures?
- How will erosion and transportation change at different times of year?

The amount of load that a river can carry varies in different sections of the river and at different times of the year.

Deposition

When a river loses its energy it cannot carry the same load, and it has to drop (or **deposit**) some material. Deposition may happen anywhere along the river's course. Larger objects, such as boulders, can be seen clearly in the bed of a river. If the load is finer material like silt or sand, it is deposited on the river bed as layers of **sediment**.

▲ A bend in the River Till in Northumberland

Things to do

- Here are some examples of erosion, transportation and deposition. Use them to fill in the table below. It has been started for you.

  collapsed bank   *boulders on the river bed*

  layers of sediment on the river bed

  mud and silt at the mouth of a river

  branches carried along   *muddy water*

  cascading water hitting the rock face

Erosion	Transportation	Deposition
collapsed bank	branches carried along	boulders on the river bed

  Add some more examples of your own to complete the table.

- Write a paragraph to explain how rivers are powerful forces in shaping the landscape. Use the words *erosion*, *transportation* and *deposition*.

Think about

- Why might a river deposit its load?
- Where is most of the erosion taking place in the photo on this page?
- Where is most of the deposition taking place?
- What do you think is the most important form of transportation here?

River valleys and waterfalls

We have seen that a river channel is a path eroded by the river's water as it flows along.

How are the parts of a river different?

Valleys
A **valley** is the name for the land on either side of a river channel. Hills and ridges, called **divides**, separate one valley from another.

The valley's shape depends on several things:
- the type of rock in the valley
- the river's energy
- how much the wind and rain have eroded the valley
- the length of time the river, wind and rain have had to work.

Think about
- Try to put the list on the right into an order of importance. Explain your order.

Valleys change shape along the length of the river – that is, along its **course**. Each valley is different, but there are general patterns in shape. Look carefully at the diagrams and work out what the pattern is.

Upper course
Near its source a river cuts a steep V-shaped valley through rock, leaving jagged divides on either side. The river channel takes up most of the valley floor. This is where you are most likely to find waterfalls and rapids.

Middle course
Here the valley floor becomes wider. The divides are lower and more rounded. The amount of water in the channel grows as more streams (called **tributaries**) join the main river.

Lower course
The river channel widens towards its mouth. The valley is broad and flat. Often the river winds across the valley in a series of bends called **meanders**. This is the part of the river that is most likely to flood.

Valleys can take many thousands of years to form.

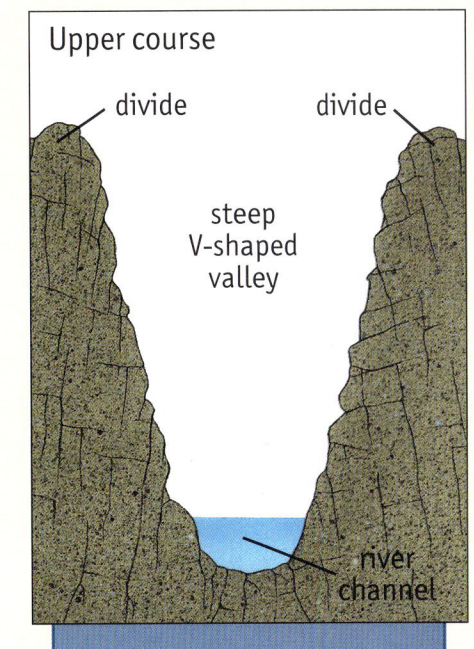

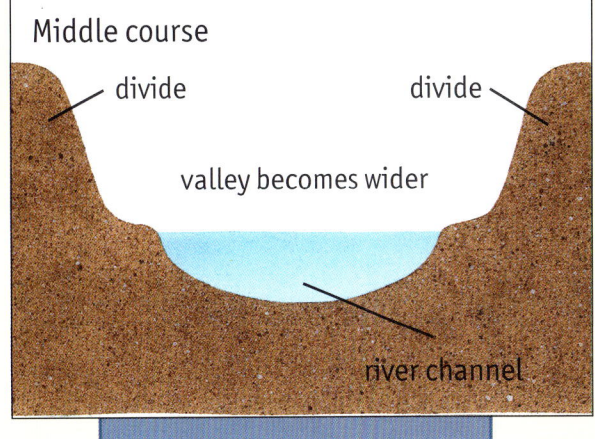

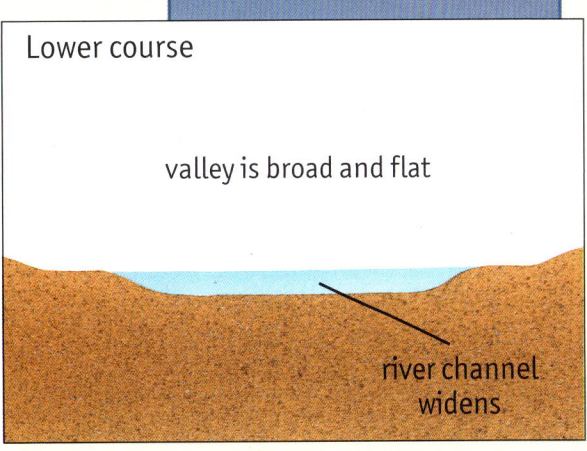

Things to do
- Copy the sketch on page 14 and label:
  *the valley sides
  the river channel
  the divides.*

15

Things to do

- Make sketches of each of photos A and B, like the one on page 14.
- In which section of the river's course is each of your three sketches?

Gorges

A **gorge** is a deep, steep-sided rocky valley.

▼ This is a gorge on the River Rhine in Germany.

▼ Area of the Rhine Gorge

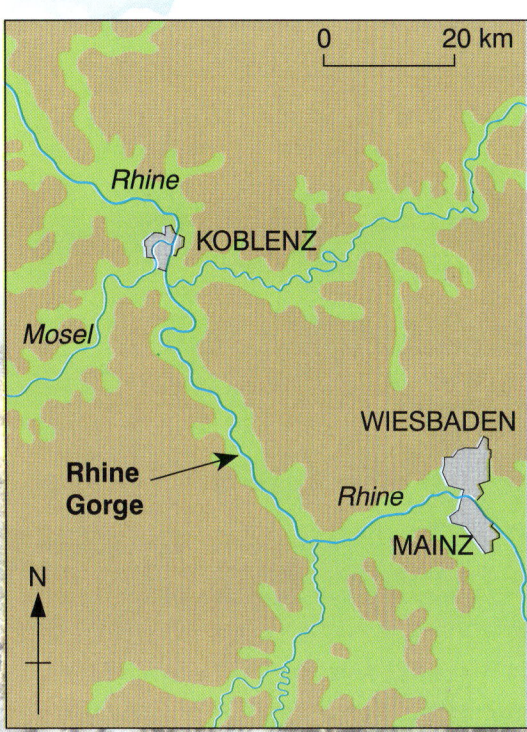

Things to find

- There are some famous examples of gorges in Britain too, for example on the Rivers Wye and Derwent. Find some other examples.
- Look for some pictures of gorges and make a display of these.

Think about

- Find the gorge on the map of the Rhine. Look at the list of things on page 14 that shape a river valley. Which of these do you think is the most important in this valley?

Waterfalls

Waterfalls form where there is a sudden drop or 'step' in the river channel. They can form for different reasons. Some are formed when the river flows from an area of hard rock to an area of soft rock.

◄ When a river flows from harder to softer rock, the softer rock gradually wears away.

◄ The water continues to erode the softer rock. The force of the water splashing back creates a plunge pool, with the harder rock overhanging it.

◄ Blocks of hard rock break off and the edge of the waterfall gradually moves upstream.

Niagara Falls in North America (shown in the background picture) formed in this way. The River Niagara flows over hard limestone rocks onto softer shales and sandstones. The water falls about 50 metres, and is wearing away the softer rocks below.

Things to do

- Find Niagara Falls in an atlas.
- Niagara Falls were formed about 10,000–12,000 years ago. They are cutting the rock back about 1.5 metres a year. How many years will it take for the Falls to move back a kilometre?
- This waterfall was formed in a different way from Niagara Falls. How do you think it was formed? Write down your ideas.

◀ A waterfall on the island of Skye, in Scotland

▲ Hardraw Force in the Pennines. This waterfall was formed in a similar way to Niagara Falls.

Things to find

- Find out the names and heights of some of the world's largest waterfalls.

Things to do

- Choose **one** of these features and make up a short information sheet on it. Use diagrams or photos and give examples.
  – River valleys
  – Gorges
  – Waterfalls

19

6

Flood plains

When a river is full, any extra water in its channel cannot be carried away, and it flows over the river's banks. When this happens the river is 'in flood'.

What happens to the landscape when a river floods?

Think about

- Why do you think a flood plain is almost level?
- What reasons can you think of for a river to flood?
- As much as a centimetre of sediment may be left on a flood plain every year. How much is that in your lifetime? How much is it in 100 years?
- What advantages and disadvantages does deposition bring?

A river in flood — sediment, river channel, flood water

When water spills over a river's bank it covers the land on either side of the channel. This flooded area is the river's **flood plain**. The river loses some of its energy and moves more slowly. It begins to drop (deposit) its load, leaving layers of sediment.

Water follows the easiest and straightest path down a slope. So why does a river bend? Scientists have spent years trying to find out why a meander begins to form. They know *what* happens, but they don't really know *why*.

Direction of flow of water

A meander starts to form. Water erodes sediment from the part of the bank where the flow is greatest. Sediment is deposited along the part of the bank where the flow is less.

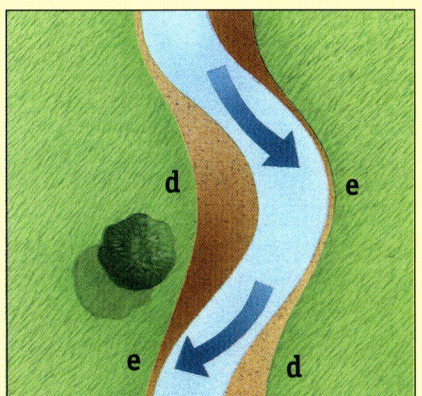

Over time, the meander becomes more distinct.

e = erosion
d = deposition

◀ The formation of a meander

Things to do

- These diagrams show what happens when a river meanders. Write a report to explain the diagrams. Use these words in your explanation:
  erosion
  transportation
  deposition
  energy
  flow
  sediment

- Draw a 'bird's-eye view' of the river in the photo opposite. Mark green crosses where there is erosion, and red crosses where there is deposition.

8

Deltas and estuaries

What happens when a river flows into the sea?

When rivers flow into the sea, **deltas** and **estuaries** are formed.

The Nile Delta

The River Nile flows northwards through Africa into the Mediterranean Sea. For thousands of years, as the river slows down where it meets the sea, it has deposited fine sediment called **silt** at its mouth.

As the river deposits the sediments, the river bed and banks slowly build up above the surrounding land. Streams of water escape from the main channel to form new channels called **distributaries**. The silt and distributaries now form a triangle-shaped area called the Nile Delta. There is a map of a delta in the Glossary.

Things to do

- Look at the photo of the Nile Delta. Use an atlas to find out the names of its two main distributaries.
- *Mississippi*
  Ganges
  Rhine
  Rhône
  Volga
  Irrawaddy
  These rivers all have deltas. Choose one, and use an atlas to draw a map of its delta. Label the river, the distributaries and the delta. Name the sea into which the river flows.

The Nile Delta

24

Estuaries

Not all rivers form deltas. Some rivers, like the Thames and the Severn, enter the sea in estuaries.

An estuary is a tidal area. At high tide the mudflats are covered with sea water. At low tide they are uncovered.

The river widens out as it flows into an estuary and meets the sea. On many estuaries there are important sea ports.

▼ This is the estuary of the River Dovey in Wales. The map shows the same area.

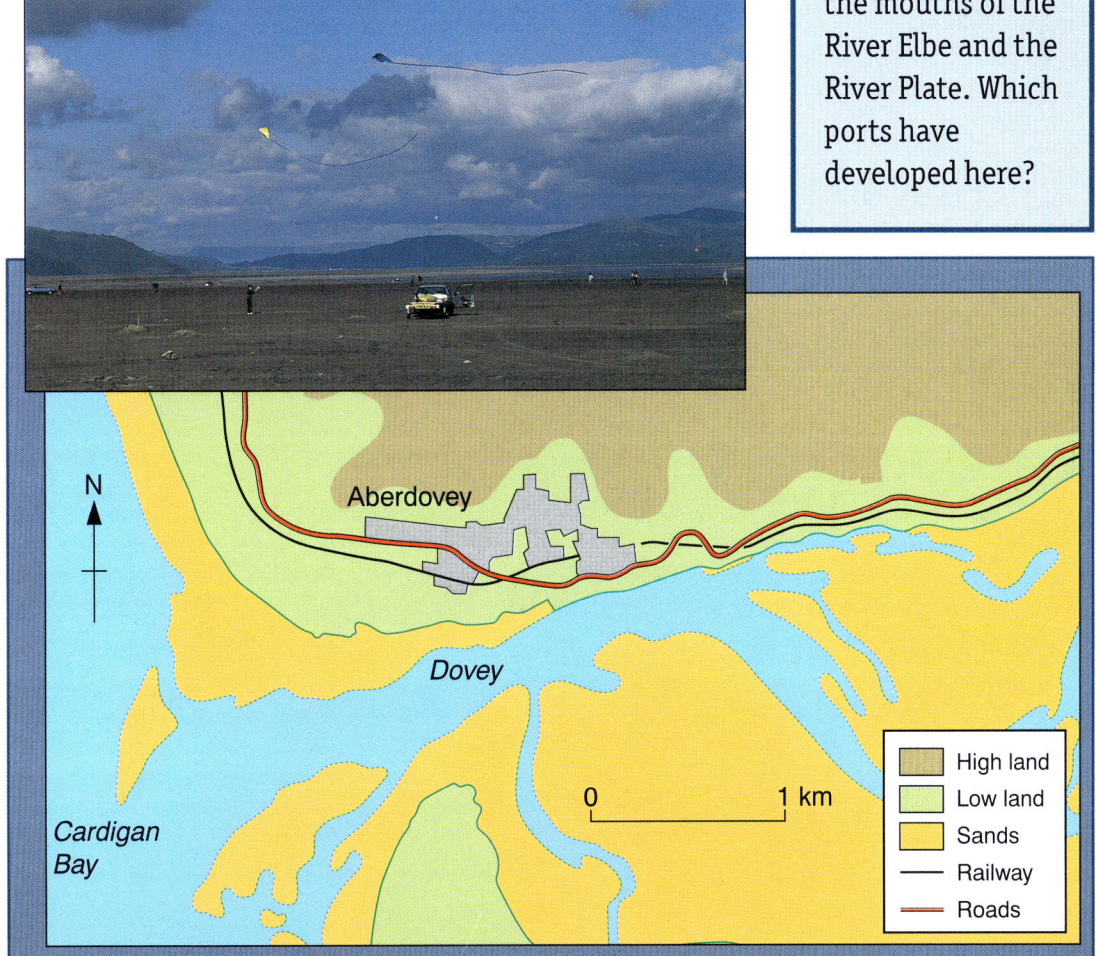

Things to find

- Was this photo taken at high tide or low tide?
- What do you think the mudflats are being used for?

Things to do

Use an atlas to find the mouths of the River Elbe and the River Plate. Which ports have developed here?

9 Rivers and industry

Why are so many industries located close to rivers?

Water is used for washing and dyeing

Water is used making chem

Water is used in making cars

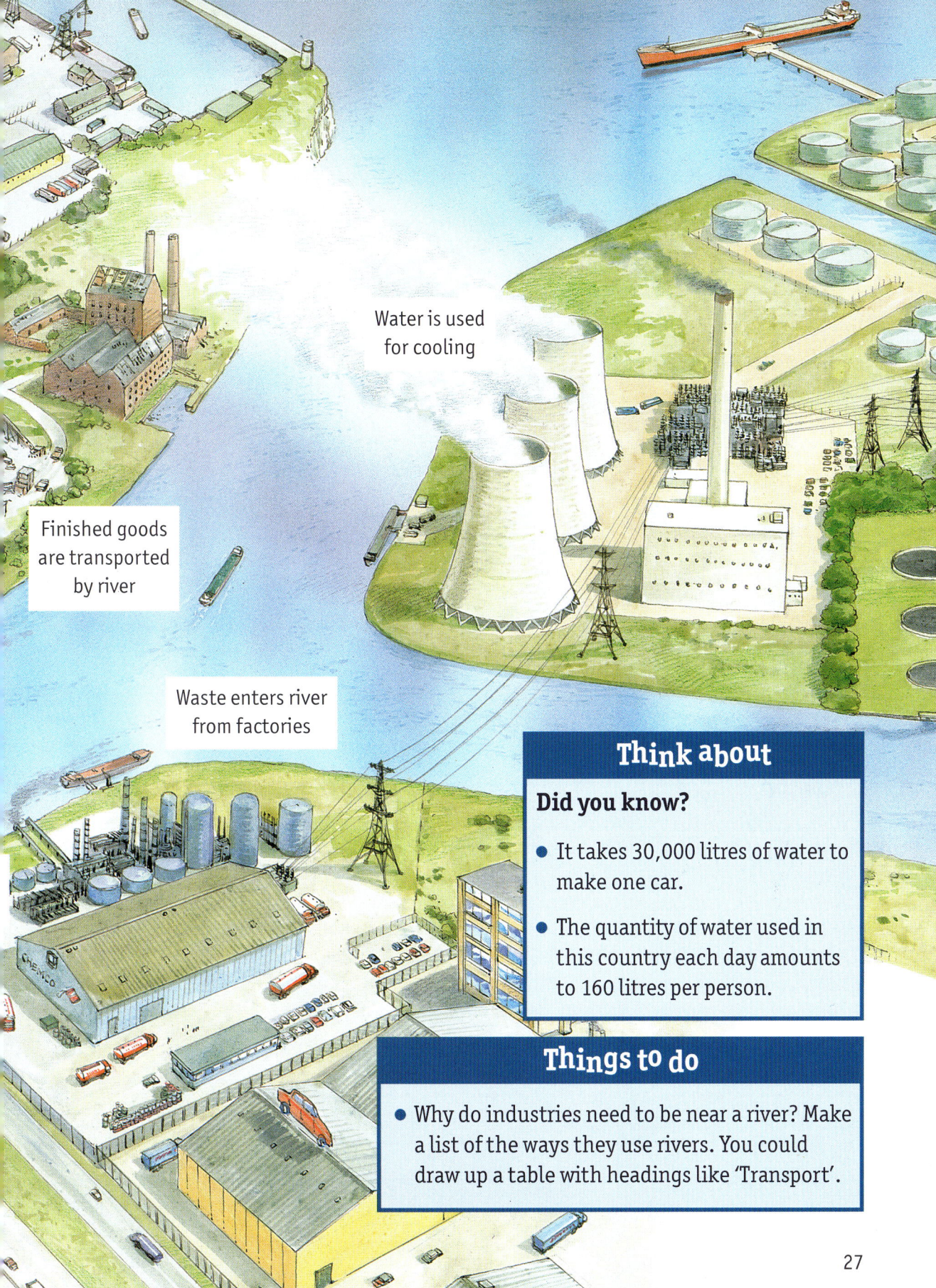

Water is used for cooling

Finished goods are transported by river

Waste enters river from factories

Think about

Did you know?

- It takes 30,000 litres of water to make one car.
- The quantity of water used in this country each day amounts to 160 litres per person.

Things to do

- Why do industries need to be near a river? Make a list of the ways they use rivers. You could draw up a table with headings like 'Transport'.

10 Enjoying rivers

People have used rivers to enjoy themselves for centuries.

Why are rivers *fun*?

Things to do

- List the recreation activities that this river is used for.
- How do you think these activities might affect the river?
- What recreational activities can the different parts of a river be used for?
- With a partner, write a set of rules on how to use a river safely and considerately. Put them in order of importance.

11 Controlling rivers

Why do we control rivers?

Clywedog Reservoir in Wales ▶

Think about

- Look at these three photos. How is the river controlled in each one?
- Why is this control needed? What happens without this control?
- Which ways of controlling rivers can be used by individuals?
- Which need lots of money, and special equipment?

Using a shaduf in the Nile Delta ▶

◀ A power station on the Niagara River

Things to do

Either
- Make a class book about types of river control that you read about or see on TV. How successful are they?

Or
- Write a newspaper account of a river in flood. You could be at the scene while it is happening, or arrive as the floodwaters begin to go down.

Even with huge and expensive engineering projects, it is not always possible to prevent river disasters. This photo shows the Mississippi floods in 1993.

Looking at a local river

What is our local river like?

You are going to plan an investigation of a river, stream, or brook near to you. You may be able to find out some things from maps and books, but you will also need to visit the river.

You will decide on the activities, and what equipment you will need to take with you.

First of all you need to think of some questions to ask about your river. Here are some ideas to help you.

1 You could take some *measurements*.
   - What will you measure?
   - How will you do this?
   - How will you make sure you are safe?
   - What will you need to take with you?

REMEMBER!

Water is a powerful force. Even shallow water can be dangerous. Make sure you follow these rules:

- Listen to instructions your teacher gives you.
- Never visit a river on your own.

2 You could *describe* parts of the river or stream and what you can see and find there.
- Think about what you have already learned in this book.
- Look for different features and examples of the processes of erosion, transportation and deposition in your river.
- Describe the river bed, the banks and the movement of the water.
- Look for different uses of the river.
- Think of a way of describing how attractive the river is – make up a list of things to look for, and decide on a way of 'scoring' your river, or different parts of it. You might give a score of 10 if the river is very clean, 1 if it is really dirty.

3 Now you need to think of ways to *record* your findings. You might use drawings and sketch maps, tables and charts, photographs and notes.

Things to do

- Design a data collection chart to take with you. It should have spaces for all the information you want to record. How will you show where your research is being carried out?

- Make a list of the equipment you will need for your investigation.

Make another visit to your river at a different time of the year. Before you carry out the second investigation, make some predictions about the results. Will they be the same or different? Why do you think this?

Ideas
Do you think the speed of the water in the river will be the same along its course? Make some predictions. Test out your ideas and try to explain your results.

Other ideas – or for bigger rivers
- Is your river important to anyone? Has the importance of the river changed? Do you think it will be important in the future?
- How is your river used for recreation?
- Has your local river been used in the past for industry? Compare its past use with present use. How have things changed?
- Is your river used for transport?

Think of the best ways to write up your investigation. You could make a class display, or make books about your river or stream.

13 Some great world rivers

What makes a river *special*?

The Yellow River

Think about

- What advantages and disadvantages do you think the Yellow River brings to the Chinese people?
- The Yellow River is also known as 'China's Sorrow'. Why do you think it was given this name?

The Huanghe or Yellow River gets its name from the huge quantities of yellowish-grey sediment, or loess, that it transports downstream every year from its hilly middle course. It is one of the muddiest rivers in the world.

For thousands of years the Yellow River has deposited loess on its flood plain when it bursts its banks. This creates rich farming land where millions of Chinese farmers live and work. The river is used for irrigation, and supplies water for homes and factories.

During the rainy season the volume of water in the river can increase 100 times. If the river banks collapse, huge amounts of water can flood an area as large as Britain.

Disaster!

IN 1986 A CHEMICAL warehouse near Basel caught fire. As the fire was put out, over 30 tonnes of toxic chemicals were washed into the Rhine. Fish were killed as far away as 100 km downstream. After this disaster, the Rhine Action Programme was formed to clean up the river. Read about the changes and improvements that have been made. ▶

As a result of these changes, by 1990 some salmon had returned to the river, and now there are at least 40 fish species living in the river.

Things to do

- Explain how salmon in the Rhine would have been affected by: *power stations*, *chemical factories*, *farms*, *building of barrages*.
- The Rhine is still a polluted river. Write a letter to the Director of the Rhine Action Programme suggesting other ways of improving the quality of the river.

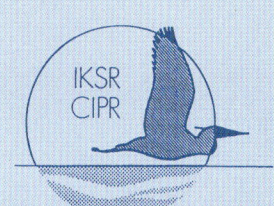

Rhine Action Programme

Aims
- to ensure that species like the salmon return to the river
- to make sure the Rhine can be used for drinking water
- to reduce toxic chemicals in the river.

Improvements
- an accident alarm system
- monitoring of pollution levels
- less toxic waste from factories
- limits on the water temperature
- replanting along the river banks
- fish ladders beside the barrages
- new sewage works.

The magnificent Severn

The Severn is the longest river in Great Britain. It flows from the Welsh mountains to the Bristol Channel, a distance of about 350 km. The photos on these pages show different parts of the Severn.

▼ The course of the River Severn

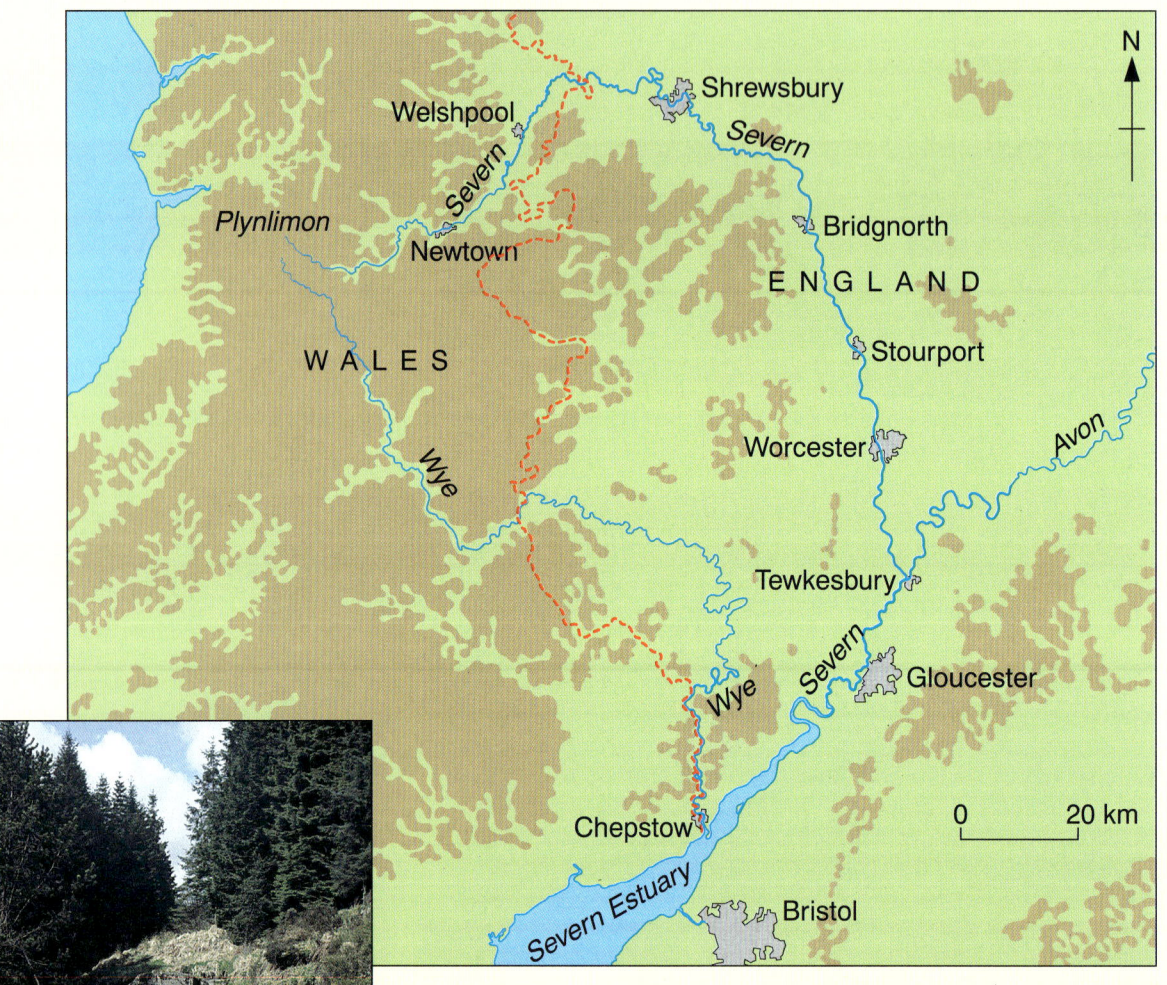

The Severn is a clean river. It is called a 'first-class' river by the Environment Agency.

For some of its course the river flows in a steep-sided rocky valley. At other times it meanders through a gently-sloping valley. Below Gloucester, the Severn widens out into an estuary.

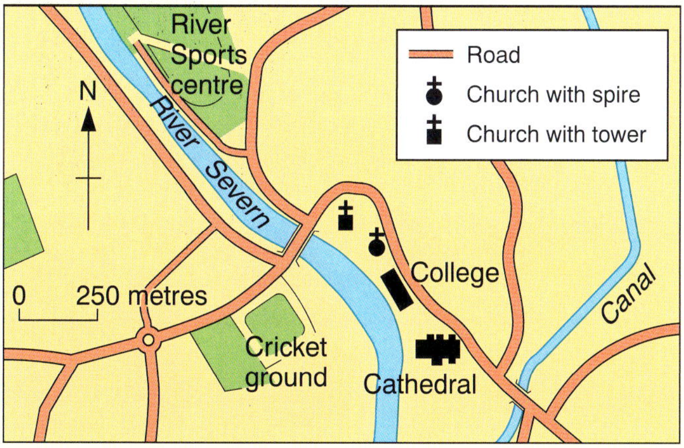

Things to do

- Describe what the river and its valley is like in each picture.

- Where in the river's course do you think each photo was taken? Explain your answers.

- List the towns along the Severn.

◀ This map shows one of the photo locations. Which one?

As you have seen in the rest of this book, rivers are important to us for many reasons. All these people use the River Severn.

A fisherman

"Almost every type of British freshwater fish is found here."

A bird-watcher

"The banks of the Severn are beautiful to walk along, and if you're lucky you might see a kingfisher."

Boatman of the *Severn Belle*

"In the summer lots of people like to travel in my boat along the Severn."

Conclusion

Why are rivers so important to us?

In this book you have found out about rivers – about the work they do, about how they are similar and how they are different. You have also learned how people use rivers, and about the problems rivers can bring.

Things to do

- Look at each of the photos on these pages. In which section of a river might you find these activities taking place? Explain your answer.

- Make a list of other river activities. Compare your answer with others in your class.

- Now draw a diagram to show what you know about rivers. You could make your diagram look like a river with tributaries.

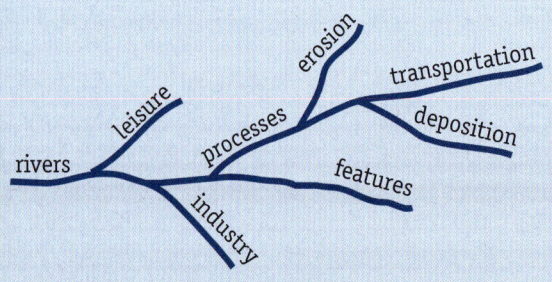

Think about

- Look back at the list of ideas about rivers you made when you started to read this book. Compare that list with what you have learned. How have your ideas about rivers changed?

45

Glossary

channel ▶
the path formed by flowing water through which a river or stream flows

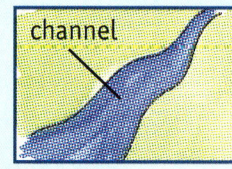

course
the path followed by a river or stream from its source to its mouth

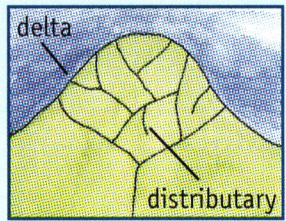

◀ **delta**
a triangular or fan-shaped deposit of sediment formed at the mouth of a river

deposition
the dropping of the sediment carried by a river

▲ **distributary**
a stream or river flowing from the main channel through the deposits of sediment in a delta

divide ▶
an area of high ground separating two river basins

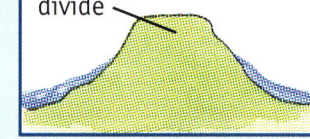

erosion
the wearing away of rock and soil by running water – one of the processes at work in a river

estuary ▶
the wide tidal area at the mouth of a river where it reaches the sea, and where fresh and salt water mix. A unique environment for wildlife, and an ideal site for a port

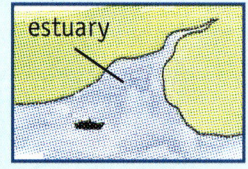

flood plain ▶
flat land at the side of a river where flooding takes place. The floods deposit fertile sediments which make the area into rich farming land

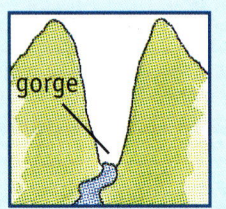

◀ **gorge**
a deep, narrow river valley usually formed when the river erodes downwards quickly

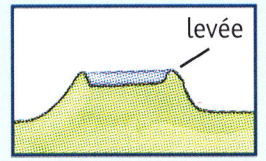

◀ **levée**
a bank built up by a river along the edges of its channel from sediments deposited during flooding. Sometimes artificial levées are built along rivers to protect land from flooding

load ▶
the material (sand, mud, rock, chemicals) carried along by a river

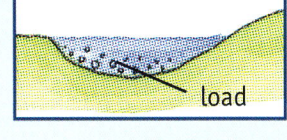

meander ▶
a curve or wide loop in the middle or lower parts of a river

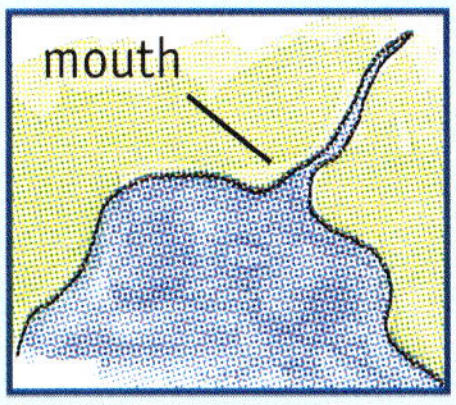

◀ **mouth**
the end of a river where it joins another river, a lake or a sea

river basin/drainage area
the area drained by a river and all its tributaries

sediment
tiny pieces of rock in the form of sand, silt and clay eroded by the river

silt
a sort of sediment carried by a river, made up of particles smaller than sand and larger than clay

source ▶
the point at which a river starts

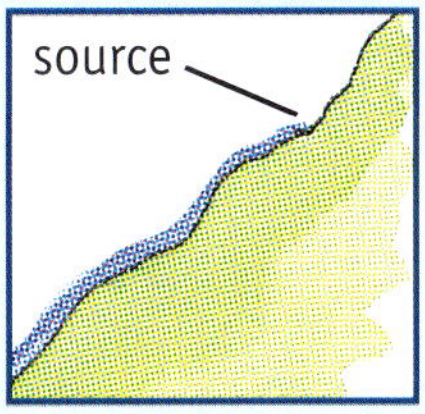

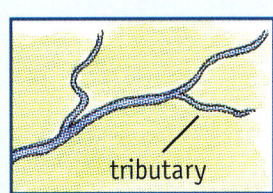

spring
a natural flow of water from the ground

transportation
the carrying along of material – one of the processes at work in a river

tributary ▶
a small stream or river that joins a large one

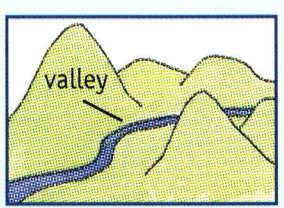

◀ **valley**
a low area between hills, usually containing a stream or river and formed by the erosion of the running water

Index

C channel, 10, 14–15, 18, 20, 21, 22, 24
course, 12, 15, 22

D delta, 24
deposition, 10, 12–13, 20, 23
distributary, 24
divide, 14, 15

E energy, 10, 14, 20, 23
erosion, 10, 11, 13, 14, 23
estuary, 25, 40

F farming, 36, 43
flood, 15, 20–21, 31, 36
flood plain, 20–21, 36

G gorge, 17

I industry, 26–27, 36, 38–39
irrigation, 36

L landscape, 2, 10
levée, 21
load, 11, 13

M meander, 15, 22–23, 40
Mississippi, 21, 24, 31
mouth, 7, 8, 15

N Niagara, 18, 30
Nile, 24, 30

P permeable rocks, 6, 9
pollution, 38–39

R rapids, 15
recreation, 28–29, 42
Rhine, 9, 17, 24, 38–39
river basin/drainage area, 8–9

S sediment, 13, 20, 21, 23, 24, 36
Severn, 25, 40–43
silt, 24
source, 6, 8, 15
spring, 6

T Thames, 25
transport, 38, 42
transportation, 10, 11–12, 23
tributary, 15

V valley, 14–17, 40, 41

W waterfall, 15, 18–19

Y Yellow River, 36–37